Special Diets

Dairy-Free Diets

by Mari Schuh

Consulting Editor: Gail Saunders-Smith, PhD

Consultant:
Amy L. Lusk, MS, RD, LD
Registered Dietitian

CAPSTONE PRESS
a capstone imprint

Pebble Plus is published by Capstone Press,
1710 Roe Crest Drive, North Mankato, Minnesota 56003.
www.capstonepub.com

The author dedicates this book to her niece Cami Schuh of Mankato, Minnesota.

Library of Congress Cataloging-in-Publication Data
Schuh, Mari C., 1975– author.
Dairy-free diets / by Mari Schuh
    pages cm.—(Pebble plus. Special diets)
  Summary: "Simple text and full-color photographs give an overview of a dairy-free diet"—Provided by publisher.
  Audience: Age 4-8.
  Audience: Grades K to 3.
  Includes bibliographical references and index.
ISBN 978-1-4914-0590-1 (library binding)
ISBN 978-1-4914-0624-3 (ebook pdf)
1. Milk-free diet—Juvenile literature. 2. Dairy substitutes—Juvenile literature. I. Title.

RM234.5.S38 2015
641.3'02—dc23

2013050809

Editorial Credits
Shelly Lyons, editor; Heidi Thompson, designer; Kelly Garvin, media researcher;
Katy LaVigne, production specialist

Photo Credits
All photos by Capstone Studio/Karon Dubke

Note to Parents and Teachers

The Special Diets series supports national science standards related to health and nutrition. This book describes and illustrates some foods that fit and don't fit into a dairy-free diet. The images support early readers in understanding the text. The repetition of words and phrases helps early readers learn new words. This book also introduces early readers to subject-specific vocabulary words, which are defined in the Glossary section. Early readers may need assistance to read some words and to use the Table of Contents, Glossary, Read More, Internet Sites, and Index sections of the book.

Printed in the United States of America in North Mankato, Minnesota.
032014   008087CGF14

Table of Contents

Who Needs a Dairy-Free Diet?

Some people can't eat cheese, milk, or other dairy foods. They have milk allergies or intolerances. There are many foods they can eat.

Eat This, Not That

Instead of cow's milk,

people can drink soy milk.

Rice milk is fine too.

Some smoothies are made
with milk or yogurt.
People can make
a dairy-free smoothie
with fruit, ice, and juice.

Sorbet makes a great treat
instead of ice cream.
It's made with fruit,
juice, and sugar.

People who can't eat dairy
can eat plenty of healthy foods.
Fruits, vegetables, meats,
and grains make great snacks.

Many foods are made with milk.

Adults who know about

food allergies can read labels.

They can check to see

if food is safe to eat.

What's a Reaction?

People with food allergies

may have an allergic reaction.

They might throw up.

They may get hives or

have trouble breathing.

If someone has an allergic reaction,
get help right away.
They need medicine quickly.
Tell an adult and call 911.

Be a Good Friend

Kids who can't eat dairy

like to play and have fun.

Help them stay away from dairy.

You'll make a new friend!

Safe Recipe Trail Mix

What You Need

1 cup (240 mL) sunflower seeds
1 cup (240 mL) mixed nuts
1 cup (240 mL) dried fruit
1 cup (240 mL) cereal or granola
1 cup (240 mL) mini pretzels
1 cup (240 mL) raisins

What You Do

Mix all ingredients together.
Put in a container with a tight lid.
Keep at room temperature.

Glossary

allergic—when something, like food or a bee sting, makes someone feel very sick

allergic reaction—the body's response when a person with a food allergy breathes in, touches, or eats a certain food; a reaction may cause an upset stomach, hives, breathing problems, and other problems

dairy—having to do with milk products

food allergy—a condition that makes people very sick when they breathe in, touch, or eat a certain food

hive—an itchy spot or red patch on the skin caused by an allergy or illness

intolerance—not being able to eat certain foods without becoming ill

label—a list on food wrappers that shows what the food is made of

rice milk—a kind of milk made from rice; rice milk is usually made from brown rice

soy milk—a kind of milk made from soybeans

Read More

Landau, Elaine. *Food Allergies*. Head-to-Toe Health. Tarrytown, N.Y.: Marshall Cavendish Benchmark, 2010.

Olson, Gillia M. *MyPlate and You*. Health and Your Body. Mankato, Minn.: Capstone Press, 2012.

Wethington, Julie. *Yes I Can!: Have My Cake and Food Allergies Too*. Columbia, MD: DragonWing Books, 2012.

Internet Sites

FactHound offers a safe, fun way to find Internet sites related to this book. All of the sites on FactHound have been researched by our staff.

Here's all you do:
Visit *www.facthound.com*
Type in this code: 9781491405901

Index

Super-cool stuff! Check out projects, games and lots more at **www.capstonekids.com**

Critical Thinking Using the Common Core

1. Healthy foods are an important part of a dairy-free diet. What are some healthy foods that you can include in your diet? (Key Ideas and Details)

2. Some people are allergic to dairy. If you see someone having an allergic reaction, what should you do? (Key Ideas and Details)

Word Count: 180
Grade: 1
Early-Intervention Level: 16